# Snake Hill

Volume I

The Nineteenth Century

A Societal Look at Snake Hill which served Hudson County
for more than 100 years and then disappeared

by

Linda L. Stampoulos

CCB Publishing
British Columbia, Canada

Snake Hill Volume I The Nineteenth Century:
A Societal Look at Snake Hill Which Served Hudson County
for More Than 100 Years and Then Disappeared

Copyright ©2015 by Linda L. Stampoulos
ISBN-13  978-1-77143-235-1
First Edition

Library and Archives Canada Cataloguing in Publication
Stampoulos, Linda L., 1946-, author
Snake Hill volume I the nineteenth century : a societal look at Snake Hill which served Hudson County for more than 100 years and then disappeared / by Linda L. Stampoulos. -- First edition.
Issued in print and electronic formats.
ISBN 978-1-77143-234-4 (hbk.).--ISBN 978-1-77143-235-1 (pbk.).--ISBN 978-1-77143-236-8 (pdf)
Additional cataloguing data available from Library and Archives Canada

For all general information regarding other books by Linda L. Stampoulos, visit pompanobooks.com

Extreme care has been taken by the author to ensure that all information presented in this book is accurate and up to date at the time of publishing. Neither the author nor the publisher can be held responsible for any errors or omissions. Additionally, neither is any liability assumed for damages resulting from the use of the information contained herein.

All rights reserved. No part of this publication may be reproduced, stored in a retrieval system or transmitted in any form or by any means, electronic, mechanical, photocopying, recording or otherwise without the express written permission of the publisher.

Publisher:  CCB Publishing
            British Columbia, Canada
            www.ccbpublishing.com

# For Ella

*A Slight Token of Love and Remembrance*

# Books by Linda L. Stampoulos

*Visiting the Grand Canyon, Views of Early Tourism*

*The Redemption of Black Elk*

*Black Elks Vermachtnis*

*Two on a Bridge*
(Guidebook & Workbook)

*Snake Hill Volume I The Nineteenth Century*

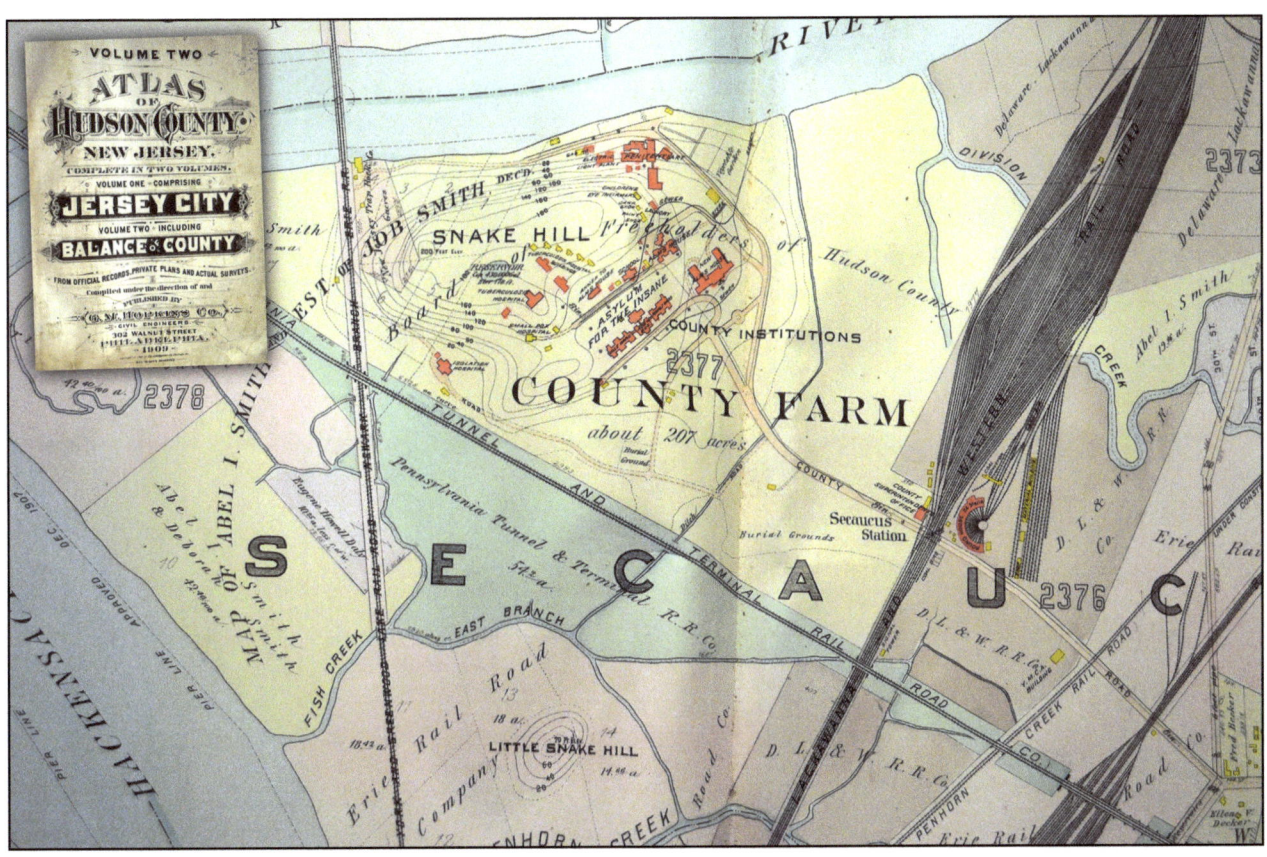

A 1909 map of Snake Hill, *Atlas of Hudson County New Jersey, Volume Two*, G.M. Hopkins Co. Philadelphia, Pa. Daniel Van Winkle mentions a reference in *History of the Municipalities of Hudson County, New Jersey 1630-1923*, "Secaucus is an island in the cedar swamp of the Hackensack River, in Bergen Township, Bergen County. It is nearly four miles long by half a mile wide, terminating in a very distinguished elevation called Snake Hill."

# Contents

Introduction ..................................................................................... 1

One Road ......................................................................................... 4
The Almshouses: Old and New ...................................................... 13
The Penitentiary ............................................................................. 29
The Lunatic Asylum ....................................................................... 47
The Infectious Disease Hospitals ................................................... 67
The Look Homeward ..................................................................... 83

References ...................................................................................... 90
Acknowledgements ........................................................................ 92
About the Author ........................................................................... 93

# Introduction

A solitary flagpole stands high on a hill overlooking the skyline of Manhattan marking the site that once was home to thousands of individuals: prisoners; patients suffering from mental and infectious diseases; and the homeless families of Hudson County. This area known as Snake Hill lies in the southern portion of the Town of Secaucus, totally surrounded by water and salt marsh. Its oasis of rich farmland rises from the meadowlands less than 15 minutes from Times Square. Travelers on the Eastern Spur of the New Jersey Turnpike near Exit 15X are familiar with Snake Hill's landmark rock formation often painted with college fraternity symbols on its eastern slope. Once made aware of it, one might catch a glimpse of a lonely smokestack, a remaining monument, standing tribute to the facility that served Hudson County for more than a hundred years.

As time passed and the buildings on "the Hill" disappeared, the only surviving memories involve stories told about the lunatic asylum. Actually, there were many other services that existed years before the asylum was built including an almshouse and a penitentiary.

There are many 19th century references to Snake Hill's beauty and uniqueness.

Daniel Van Winkle reported in his *History of the Municipalities of Hudson County, New Jersey 1630-1923*:

> Snake Hill is properly named. The Indians called it by that name which means "the home of the snakes" and all the early colonists gave the place a wide birth notwithstanding that its wood-crowned heights sheltered many acres of productive soil. They kept away because the marshland was literally infested with huge black water snakes, many of them twelve to fifteen feet long.

Perhaps one of the more colorful descriptions comes from the *New-York Daily Tribune*, November 1850 Geological and Topographical View of New Jersey that reads:

> There is an island which is sometimes called *Secaucus*, situated between three and four miles north-east of Jersey City, and which, like adjacent shores, is chiefly composed of red and gray sandstone. At the end of this hill is an elevated height or promontory, which presents a view of unsurpassed magnificence. This elevation on the south end, which is recognized by the name "Snake Hill" assumes a conical form, and is composed of trap rock resting upon sandstone.
>
> The lover of the romantic, as he stands upon its verdure-clad summit, can survey, almost at its base, the sparkling waters of the Passaic and Hackensack Rivers. He can also see on the western side beautiful ranges of mountains and populous towns; on the east the dingy, noisy, and bustling City of New York, and hear its bells tremble on the surrounding atmosphere, as their sounds reverberate from hill to hill and mingle in the air above. On the south, the broad bosom of the mighty ocean stretches away in all its grandeur, far as the eye can reach.

Its name changed from Snake Hill to Laurel Hill in 1926, when a Hudson County Freeholder called it the "crowning Laurel of Hudson County" because of its prominence in the low lying salt marsh. Although it has been officially changed, many local residents and even traffic reporters still call it *Snake Hill* in their discussions and geographical references.

During the 19th century, society's approach to its sick, poor and other dependents was a mirror of the culture in general. A major part of this benevolence was consideration for the plight of the patient and how he was referenced. Therefore the author cautions the reader to be prepared for the terminology used during this time period. Newspaper articles and other reports make reference to such terms as lunatics, paupers, and maniacs. To accurately present a portrait of society and at the risk of offending the reader, the language used in this book is within its historical context and was considered socially acceptable.

Presented within this volume is a societal look at the area's approach to dependent persons. Using a wide lens that comprises New York City, Newark, and Philadelphia, the reader is given a picture of the care and treatment provided in the 19th century. In order to add a human element to these times, actual newspaper articles written over 150 years ago travel back in time to present personal stories as if they were happening now. The articles were selected for their unique ability to demonstrate the cooperation and integration of all the services on the Hill. It was its own community and like any community, everyone had a part to play for it to continue and offer services to those most in need. All photographs, except for those current ones from the author's private collection, are vintage images from the last part of the 19th century.

One by one, the services were moved to other locations in Hudson County. Today, the buildings have disappeared, many of the burial grounds are unmarked and forgotten, and even the land has largely been obliterated by quarrying, yet Snake Hill has a story to tell. Volume One of this series offers a look the facility's beginnings in the 19th century. It was a time when the New York metropolitan area had many dependent souls whose situation in life in some way, brought them to "the Hill," and like the buildings that once housed them, they too have disappeared.

# Chapter One

## One Road

Figure 1.1 There was one road leading from Jersey City to Snake Hill, and for many, it became a one-way road. The trip for anyone wanting to visit a loved one could take an entire day or longer. (Photograph courtesy the Dan McDonough Collection)

In the first half of the 19th century, there weren't many institutions that addressed the many specific needs of the destitute and dependent populations. Often the sick and mentally ill were mixed with the elderly, abandoned children, and even criminals. Hudson County looked for available land to care for its homeless and its poor, and they found it at Snake Hill.

According to Daniel Van Winkle's *History of the Municipalities of Hudson County, New Jersey 1630-1923*:

> The poor of the town (Secaucus) in the early days were farmed out to those who would care for them at the least expense to the township. With the increase of population it was realized that general provision must be made for the care of the poor and unfortunate of the township, and the purchase of a suitable locality for the purpose was decided upon. The Pinhorn plantation at Secaucus was said to contain in 1729 about 600 acres of timber land, 200 acres cleared land, 1,000 acres meadow, new house and barn, and two orchards of about 1,200 bearing apple trees, and some 300 acres of this plantation were taken for the "poor house farm."
> 
> The county of Hudson was carved out of the county of Bergen in 1840…An act passed by State Legislature on March 7, 1861, appointing commissioners "to provide for the sale of the poor house and farm" Purchase the area of the property at Snake Hill concluded February, 1862, the county becoming the owner."
> 
> Preparations were immediately made for the erection of the almshouse…In 1863 the building was completed. The accommodation of the building was for over 500 inmates and was first class.

Van Winkle went on to write, "It was found necessary to provide for the common care and protection of the poor, and Secaucus was determined as the most suitable spot for the "Poor House Farm." This tract of land was very good for farming and was already serving as a poor farm. The County felt that with a farm a few miles from Jersey City and containing such rich farmland, the poor, or a greater part of them could earn their way, and take some burden off the Hudson County taxpayers.

In 1863, while the country was engaged in the Civil War, the County built an almshouse at Snake Hill. Later, in 1870 a penitentiary was completed. After the lunatic asylum was added in 1873, Hudson County built several infectious disease hospitals, three churches, and a power plant. At the very top of the Hill, a 430,000 gallon reservoir provided water for "state of the art" sewage management as well as steam heat for the complex.

Figure 1.2 This is a view is of the road leading into Snake Hill. The New Almshouse can be seen on the right, and there is a glimpse of the steps leading up to the Lunatic Asylum at the end of the road. Off to the left is one of the smoke stacks on the Hill. (Photograph courtesy the Dan McDonough Collection)

Since the majority of the administrative offices for Hudson County were located in Jersey City, the county seat, as was a large amount of the population, there needed to be a convenient way to travel to the facility. There was one road leading from Jersey City to Snake Hill, and except for this road, all the institutions at the Hill provided their services in isolation. This seclusion deterred orphan boys staying at the Almshouse from running away. Anyone wanting to run away was soon discouraged by the harsh journey awaiting them through the salt marsh. In fact, travel for anyone wanting to visit a loved one could take an entire day or longer.

Figure 1.3 The road leaving "the Hill" is lined with trees. A stone archway showed the way home for some; sadly, others never would leave. (Photograph courtesy the Dan McDonough Collection)

Caring for the poor was always a costly service for larger cities. People living in the countryside had their animals and crops to provide food for their families and neighbors in need. The Almshouse produced a source of labor; adult paupers were put to work within the institutions and on the farm. The facility had over 100 acres of farmland, barns, stables, and even a blacksmith shop. Nearly all the food was raised and processed at Snake Hill.

Figure 1.4 At the entrance to Snake Hill, photograph shows two men arriving in their horse-drawn wagon, and a third waiting to greet them. (Photograph courtesy the Dan McDonough Collection)

Farming in Secaucus and the Snake Hill area was always productive. Among the crops grown were cabbage, grain and hay. The food supplied the inmates and patients and was sold in the surrounding Hudson County area as well as in New York City. Warden Warren who was in charge of the Almshouse was quoted in a 1877 newspaper as saying, "As far as the food is concerned, they have good meat or fish every day in the week, and the cabbage and vegetables …are raised right here on the hill, and is as fine as can be obtained in Washington Market." In addition to an assortment of garden vegetables, of particular importance was the hay and clover that was used to feed horses.

Figure 1.5 Perched high on the hill is the Administration Building for the Tuberculosis Department. In the front are some of the pigs raised at the Hill. According to Van Winkle, "the soil was good and the farm crops consisted of garden vegetables of all kinds, there are also several dairy and pig raising farms on the outskirts." (Photograph courtesy the Dan McDonough Collection)

From the time its first building was completed in 1863, until the middle of the 20th century, Snake Hill, like similar government facilities was dependent upon unpaid inmate labor to sustain its operations. As for those in the Lunatic Asylum, many in the 19th century felt that the proper approach to care for the insane was a greater emphasis on nature and less dependence on medicine. The exercise and fresh air was a good form of "treatment."

Figure 1.6 Inmates of the Almshouse and some of the quieter and harmless patients from the Lunatic Asylum worked the farm. It was believed that this would be a favorable activity for health and recovery. (Photograph courtesy the Dan McDonough Collection)

The eastern and northern sides of Snake Hill were dotted with its many hospitals, the penitentiary, and the almshouses for the poor and destitute. A smooth hard road stretched down the eastern hillside to the swamp, and then an artificial road made its way through the salt marsh. The acres of farmland were on the northern side of the grounds, as were many barns and outbuildings.

Figure 1.7 Various trades were carried on for the production of food by the inmates of both the Almshouse and the Penitentiary. Van Winkle wrote "the bread bakery is a noteworthy feature, being conducted on hygienic principles with separate machinery for mixing and forming loaves of bread without coming in contact with the hands. These industries are all operated by the inmates of the institutions, supervised by the proper officers." (Photograph courtesy the Dan McDonough Collection)

The 1909 map of Snake Hill depicts the layout of its buildings and shows that there were at least two areas designated as burial grounds. After spending decades in the institutions most patients lost contact with their families and the communities from which they came. When they died, they were buried with a number, not a name, and were soon forgotten.

Figure 1.8 Today, the old road still exists but leads to nowhere. A fence prevents visitors to Laurel Hill Park from trespassing into areas that are not designated as walking trails. (Photograph from the author's private collection, April 2013)

# Chapter Two

## The Almshouses: Old and New

"The cold and cheerless winter is coming on us again; many, very many of the wretched and miserable creatures who have no homes, no friends to cherish them in their feebleness and old age, devoid of sound intellect, lame and blind, go dragging out their pitiful existence over our thoroughfares, begging from door to door, and die upon our streets or in some miserable hovel, or are cast into the Almshouse, where pride whithers and the body wastes away in dark oblivion." *1856 Report, Board of Guardians of the Poor of the City and Districts of Philadephia.*

Historically local governments approached the poor as their responsibility and considered them wards of the State and their dependents rather than individuals in need of care. However, discussions of these concerns had more to do with the politics and economics of these conditions, rather than addressing the cause and treatment of such ills.

Figure 2.1 The architecture of the Almshouse, built in 1863, reflected a sense of order and responsibilty. Slightly hidden from view, the words "Hudson County Almshouse" are printed in front. (Photograph courtesy the Dan McDonough Collection)

Attention was first drawn to the poor. Immigrants were arriving in large numbers bringing with them an inability to speak English as well as diseases that were plaguing Europe at this time. Few had friends or relatives in America and most found themselves without the skills needed in an urban society. The New York metropolitan area in particular experienced an influx of large numbers of immigrants having Ellis Island serve as the gateway to America for so many. Efforts were made to prevent pauperism among newly arrived immigrants including furnishing temporary aid in sickness and poverty, and by bringing together separated families and friends. These newcomers came with little or no money, and relied on friends and relatives to take them into their homes. Bonded by their own common language and culture, pockets of immigrants settled in neighborhoods and developed little communities complete with shops and churches representing their home countries. Unfortunately for some, their dreams of a happy and prosperous life in this New World faded away leaving them no choice but to seek help from charitable institutions.

The poor were often categorized as paupers who were defined by society as persons who were dependent and possessed a disability or misfortune brought about by such causes as idleness, vagrancy, or spiritless, social and personal degradation. It was the children of these families who suffered most. Orphans who were abandoned or otherwise homeless children were dependent on total social support. Examples of socially acceptable terminology used during this period, a 19th century register of New York City Children's Charities in the area included:

- The Colored Orphan Asylum on West 143rd Street
- Crippled Boy's Home on East 14th Street
- Idiot Asylum on Randall's Island
- The Syracuse State School for the Feeble-minded

The orphaned children who could not find aid wandered the streets or were forced to work at an early age in an "indentured" situation. Many white immigrants entered indentured servitude which was actually a form of debt bondage. Some entered on their own, others, rather than go to a debtor's prison, chose to be sold into servitude by the local authority and given to "the lowest bidder." In other words, the government paid for their servitude position; this being less expensive than caring for them in an almshouse. A legal contract agreed by both sides would state the terms of the indenture. For example, the term would usually last from two to seven years after which the servant would be free to work on his own. In return, the holder of the contract had to provide food, clothing and lodging. If they were fortunate, children would enter into a "bound apprenticeship" in which they would learn a trade. These were usually orphans or children who came from an impoverished family who could not care for them.

Figure 2.2 The plaque above its door, "Hudson County Almshouse erected A.D. 1863" welcomed the poor and needy, and provided a home for those with nowhere else to live. Van Winkle noted "the contract for the carpenter's work was awarded to James McLoughlin at $14,600, and the contract for the mason work to William C. White for $12,500." (Photograph courtesy the Dan McDonough Collection)

As Van Winkle stated, the poor of the town were farmed out to people who could care for them and such was the case of a little girl named Abson as published the *The Daily Phoenix,* (Columbia, S.C.) Wednesday, January 6, 1869:

## An Unfortunate Family

A young girl named Abson, who has for the past three months been an inmate of the Hudson County Almshouse at Snake Hill, gave birth, four days ago, to a child of negro parentage, which was found dead in a bed yesterday morning, supposed to have been smothered by its mother. The circumstances of the case are somewhat singular. About eight years ago one Abson and his wife were living on a small farm in the lower part of Bergen, New Jersey. Suddenly the wife died by poison. The husband was arrested for murder, and while lying in the Hudson County Jail, awaiting trial, committed suicide by cutting his throat. One child, a little girl six years of age, was left an orphan by the double tragedy. About a year ago, at which she was 14 years of age, the girl was sent to work on a farm in Rockaway, New Jersey. During the absence of her employer's family, a negro on the farm effected her ruin, which being discovered, and she being *enceinte*, she was sent back to Bergen, and thence to the almshouse, where the child was born and killed as stated. Coroner Warren will hold an inquest.

Unfortunately for the Abson girl, the consequences of post traumatic shock syndrome and postpartum depression were not well known in the mid-1800's.

It was in the cities that those poor and homeless would go to an almshouse for food and shelter. These paupers or "inmates" as they were called were controlled by the governing body that had to manage the population of the house and require all able-bodied men and women to earn their keep.

Figure 2.3 In its beginning years as a County facility, the Almshouse with its swelling roof and commanding situation, was one of the most conspicuous objects on the Hill. (Photograph courtesy the Dan McDonough Collection)

Among the problems that presented themselves, were food shortages, lack of proper clothing, overcrowding, disease, and mental illness. Crimes associated with poverty included vagrancy and theft. In 1906 the County recognized the shortage of space and built a second Almshouse called "The New Almshouse." It was much larger and accommodated many more "inmates" than the old Almshouse.

Figure 2.4 Rising from the surrounding farmland and salt marsh, the New Almshouse provided more space to accommodate the increasing numbers of poor and homeless. (Photograph courtesy the Dan McDonough Collection)

Since many of the inmates of almshouses were children, the overseeing government bodies often provided schools for their education. There was such a school on Snake Hill, which provided these children with enough education to become useful members of society. There were three churches as well: St. Joseph's Catholic Church, a Lutheran Church, and an Episcopal Church.

In the almshouse, all persons able to work were provided with employment suitable to their condition. If the condition of the pauper did not qualify him for some employment, something would have been found for him or her to do rather than remain idle. Almshouse ward designations reflected ability to work; women were categorized by their ability to sew and knit. Those in bad health or aged were not expected to work.

Figure 2.5 Most roads connecting the buildings on Snake Hill were lined with trees and well lighted. This view of the New Almshouse shows the sunrooms on the side of the building. (Photograph courtesy the Dan McDonough Collection)

Some of the men at the almshouse were put to work in the quarry. "Getting out stone" as it was called helped support the house. This put men to work who would have otherwise idled their time away smoking pipes and conversing together. This class of men comprised those who claim that they could support themselves, and would work if they could find it. However, not being able to obtain employment, they were forced to go to the almshouse in preference to starving. In contrast, the "lazy class" who frequently wintered at the almshouse, upon finding they would put to work at the quarry, decided rather to look outside for work where they have more liberty.

The governors of one Philadelphia almshouse reported, "By cutting off the lazy, improvident set of rum-drinking loafers, we would have a better opportunity of giving to the deserving poor, of which we have many more in our midst."

Figure 2.6 The grounds on the Hill resembled an open park, fully maintained and secure. (Photograph courtesy the Dan McDonough Collection)

Since the provision of services for the poor were so costly, the local governments instituted a welfare-like system. They realized that small amounts of payments called "out-door relief" would be less costly and preventive rather than let people go further and require the almshouse. Thus the purpose of this form of welfare was to "keep them out by a little reasonable aid in groceries, coal, and to a small extent money."

Figure 2.7 The posterior side of the New Almshouse viewing the "inmates" as they were called, resting outside. (Photograph courtesy the Dan McDonough Collection)

On Wednesday, October 24, 1877, eighteen members of a Hudson County Grand Jury conducted an "unheralded" inspection of the institutions at Snake Hill. *The Sun*, a New York City newspaper reported the findings of this inspection in an October 29th article titled, "The Miseries of Snake Hill, Plain Views of Life in one of Hudson County's Institution." Subtitle: "The Paupers who Suffer in the Almshouse awhile before Going to Potter's Field – What is Given them for Food and Medicine and Sanitary Care Very Sadly Lacking." Included in the article is an interview with the current warden at that time, Patrick Warren. It was given to a reporter for *The Sun* who also toured the almshouse on Saturday, October 27th. The article only published the results of the Almshouse inspection, since the other buildings were reported to be "in fine working order." These are the bare outlines of the picture that the Grand Jury presented of the management and condition of the Almshouse. In the following narrative, the 1877 article has been presented in a way to present both sides of the issues:

Official inspection report: (10/24) The jury entered the dining room of the children's department and presented this picture of the condition of the institution. In the dining room were about eighty unclean, unkempt children, from four to twelve years of age, eating their dinner. The children all looked sickly, pale, and weak. They sat around long, rough board tables, and in front of each was a tin basin filled with plain boiled cabbage, unseasoned and tasteless, and half a slice of sour black bread. This alone composed their dinner. The children picked the cabbage from their basins with their fingers, as no knives, forks, or spoons were provided. Two women attended the tables, one of whom, as soon as she saw the visitors, began to distribute among the little ones great iron tablespoons. A juror asked whether spoons were not furnished at every meal. "No: only spoons on soup days, twice a week."

Warden Warren: (to the reporter 10/27) Come in and I will show you around the premises and you can judge for yourself whether I have been doing my duty or not. There are over 300 children here, much too crowded. As far as the food is concerned, they have good meat or fish every day in the week, and the cabbage that the jury derided I'll bet is far better than the jury get at home. It is raised right here on the hill, and is as fine as can be obtained in Washington Market. It is always boiled with pork, and of course is properly seasoned thereby. We do not furnish coffee any longer, but good tea is had at both breakfast and supper. We also provide plenty of good milk. Our flour is good and wholesome, and our molasses, sugar and rice are first class. We do not furnish spoons and knives and forks, for the simple reason that if we did the inmates would either steal or destroy them.

Reporter: (10/27) When I arrived, the Warden had been distributing clothing to the paupers, "Hudson County Almshouse" boldly printed on each piece. I visited a dormitory with a dozen beds side by side along the walls. In a far corner, by a window, a plain pine coffin, scarcely two feet in length, rested on a bed. The lid lay nearly on the coverlid. A nurse bent over the box and arranged the folds of a clean white shroud around the dead form of a little child. "It's little Jimmy Gray," she said. "He was only ten months old, a lovely boy. There are his father and mother," pointing to a young man and woman who leaned abstractedly against the bed, "Please put his name and death in the paper, God bless you." And the nurse folded the hands of the child across each other.

Official inspection report: (10/24) The condition of the children under four years was even worse than that of the older ones. Each woman having an infant is given one pint of thin milk in the morning and another pint at night. The mortality is great among the infants, and those who are strong enough to sustain this regime are peevish and fretful.

Warden Warren: (10/27) We scrub twice every day in the week, and I don't know what that Grand Jury could see here to find fault with. I have tried hard to make the institution a success, and I thought that I had succeeded. But I can tell you the whole gist of the matter: Those fellows came up here to find fault – they came prejudiced and with malicious intentions. I happened to be away that day for the first time in two weeks, and they took that very day to make their visit. They began to find fault before they entered the building then they listened to every lie that the inmates told them. We have the very worst set of paupers of any institution in the country – the scum of Jersey City and New York. They would rather lie than tell you the truth, and if you believe all they tell you, you would think that they are actually starving. Now the truth is they are fed altogether too well, why, the warden of Blackwell's Island Almshouse said to me, after going through our building, that the inmates here have twice the amount of food that the paupers under his charge are furnished with. The quality of food here is better than that given on the island. This is also a very difficult post to fill. We have more to do in a day than most institutions in a week, and yet, while in other places like this are seven or eight officers in this there is only myself and the matron. I have been here only since July, and I thought that I succeeded admirably. Before coming here I was Warden of the Penitentiary for three years, and got along successfully. I can't understand the action of the Grand Jury, unless they have actuated by political animosity in seeking my removal. He repeated a second time that the buildings are all overcrowded and that larger quarters ought to be provided.

Official inspection report: (10/24) The entire building was unclean and the atmosphere in it was foul in the extreme. The sick are crowded into the same rooms with the well, and so limited is the medical attendance that one sick woman asserted that the physician had not visited her for five days. The physician said he was overworked, and could not pay proper attention to his patients.

Reporter: (10/27) In all the apartments were evidences of recent scrubbing, and the floors and walls shone in their neatness. In a large room is the sleeping apartment of the boys.

Warden Warren: (10/27) There were ninety-eight boys there now, not counting the seven who ran away the other day. This weather is very bad for boys and I have four or five of them down with the chills every day. That boy over there in that bed has the shakes. You can pile all the clothes on the house, and you can't keep him warm. As there are about us nasty exposed sinks in the room in which ninety-eight boys sleep, it might be suggested that something besides weather has an influence in fostering diseases.

Figure 2.8 Children played in the yard and residents rested in sunrooms and porches of the New Almshouse. Educational and religious services were important provisions for all the residents of Snake Hill, especially the children in the Almshouse. (Photograph courtesy the Dan McDonough Collection)

Unlike a soup kitchen or an emergency shelter, the inmates of the almshouse had to follow rules and give up certain freedoms if they intended to stay and receive basic needs. The County saw it absolutely necessary to enlarge accommodations for the constantly increasing numbers that presented themselves. As cities like New York and Philadelphia grew, the amount of pauperism increased proportionately. Budgets were pushed to their limits, especially during the cold winter months.

Much thought was given as to the proper way to care for the insane patients in the typical almshouse setting. They were usually isolated and locked in small cells with little or no attention paid to their condition. The consensus of opinion in the first part of the 19$^{th}$ century was that insanity was incurable and "even the mildest cases were locked in cells."

In an 1812 report responding to a request to improve these conditions, the Board governing a Philadelphia almshouse replied, "The committee must confess their conviction that the comforts of the afflicted maniacs cannot be materially improved, nor their disorder successfully contended with, while they are exposed to the chilling damps of the present lower cells; the confined situation of which must, in many cases, render useless the best directed efforts of medical skill."

Another issue that surfaced in the administration of almshouses was the possibility of the sale of the bodies that were not claimed by family or friends. Northeastern medical schools were in need of cadavers for their students. In the larger cities, the taking of bodies from the graveyard to the lecture rooms was prevalent in the mid-nineteenth century. This practice was defended by claiming it was for the advancement of medical science. If colleges must have subjects to study, and should the supply from the almshouse be cut off, bodies of persons with families would be stolen from the cemeteries and taken to dissecting rooms.

The arguments in favor of allowing medical students to use the bodies of those who died while at the almshouse included that "as paupers they were no use to society while living, there is no wrong in making them useful when dead." A rebuttal argument to this thought was "what of those who worked and provided all their lives until now, when poverty struck."

In one typical almshouse in Philadelphia, the handling of the bodies was left to the ferryman. Located along the Delaware River, Philadelphia almshouses took advantage of the ferry system for transportation, as well as using the water for their steam heat boilers. Once the ferry was abolished, the ferryman kept his other responsibilities as well as his title. The duties of the ferryman included: supervising the engine by which the water was pumped into the buildings; taking charge of the banks of the river; overseeing the paupers in the quarry; and most importantly, attending to the duties of the graveyard. It is most probable that a similar position, if not so named, existed at Snake Hill.

During this period in Philadelphia, medical students were charged from ten to fifteen dollars for each human subject for the dissecting tables. A brisk business was done during the terms of the college lectures in the corpses of those who died at the almshouse and whose bodies were not claimed by friends. It should be noted that the City of Philadelphia never profited from the sale of these bodies, but all indications lead to the inference that the ferryman received some payment. The Board of Guardians which was directly responsible for almshouse operations always denied any "traffic in human corpses" especially since the proceeds did not benefit the City. In addition, the Board had a vault built to hold the bodies until such time as they were claimed by family or friends, or until decay had so far progressed as to render them useless for the purposes of dissection.

Always a cause of concern was the number of drunkards and vagrants supported in the almshouses. It seemed necessary to separate the poor and needy from the drifter and the criminal. More and more the need surfaced for a house of correction to serve as the proper alternative for these populations.

The Hudson County Board of Chosen Freeholders saw the need to separate these groups and serve them in separate departments that addressed their specific needs. One of the first decisions was to remove the criminals and the criminally insane from the almshouse population and build a penitentiary to house the County's criminals.

Figure 2.9 The overgrown foundation, all that remains of the New Almshouse at Snake Hill. (Photograph from the author's private collection, April, 2013)

# Chapter Three

# The Penitentiary

"The exterior of a solitary prison should exhibit as much as possible great strength and convey to the mind of a criminal indicative of the misery which awaits the unhappy being who enters within its walls." *Minutes of the March 26, 1822 Meeting of the Board of Commissioners*, Eastern Penitentiary, Philadelphia

In 1863, the Almshouse was situated at the foot of Snake Hill somewhere near the center of the property. The Penitentiary was next to be built. The site selected was on the far side of the Hill very near the banks of the Hackensack River. On August 9, 1866 a contract for the building was awarded to Peter Doyle and David Ewling for a total cost of $83,456. Work began shortly after, and the building was completed in 1870. Patrick Warren was appointed the first keeper of the Penitentiary and Michael Kinney, convicted of breaking and entry and larceny, was the first inmate admitted.

Figure 3.1 This photograph of the Hudson County Penitentiary at Snake Hill, built in 1870, exhibits strength and security and portrays an example of Gothic architecture of the 19$^{th}$ century. (Photograph courtesy the Dan McDonough Collection)

Figure 3.2 The building's style represented its purpose; it offered a sense of order in the County's criminal justice system. (Photograph courtesy the Dan McDonough Collection)

By the time the Penitentiary at Snake Hill was completed in 1870, society was already in the midst of reviewing its approaches to incarceration and penal reform. Prior to this time, earlier in the 19th Century, prisons were built with individual cells for separate and solitary confinement. The tiny cells had inadequate ventilation, heating and plumbing. Because no regimen of activity had been developed, many prisoners suffered from mental illness and poor health.

The Quakers of Philadelphia introduced their philosophy which considered imprisonment the best for reform of the prisoner and not a time of punishment. To transform him into a productive member of society, he first must be penitent and ready to change. This would require he be isolated for long periods of time and thereby given the opportunity to reflect on his past behavior and seek penance. However, during these periods of isolation, he would be given tasks to perform to develop a skill and to keep his mind active. As French representative, Gustave de Beaumont, stated after observing the Quaker model, "Can there be a combination more powerful for reformation than of a prison which hands over the prisoner to all the trials of solitude, leads him from reflection to remorse, while it makes him industrious in his solitude."

This progressive thought was not widely accepted by those in the criminal justice system. Many thought it unfair that lawbreakers were allowed to rest all day, supported by hardworking, honest citizens. Subsequently, New York and other states abandoned absolute confinement in cells for a modified system that combined day work outside the cells and night confinement with one or two in a cell. This was the system that was adopted at Snake Hill. Its combination of working and solitude was able to prove to the prisoners that labor had a curative and moral value, and work would teach them the "habits of industry" and at the same time help defray the cost of their incarceration.

At Snake Hill, the inmates participated in the day to day responsibilities of the Penitentiary. Some worked in the quarry, while others baked bread. Bakery wagons picked up the bread which was delivered to nearby Secaucus, Jersey City and even to New York City.

Figure 3.3 Pictured is view of the grounds with Hackensack River in the background. Today, the skyline of Newark would be rising from the salt marsh. (Photograph courtesy the Dan McDonough Collection)

The population of the Penitentiary at Snake Hill included immigrants from several European countries. In 1873 there were a total of 398 committed to the Penitentiary, 310 were males and 88 were women. Of these, were 270 foreign born.

Charities in the New York City area attempted to establish a committee designed to prevent pauperism. One of their main concerns was the increasing number of imported criminals. Having an organization to detect and turn back the flow of criminals to their home countries would help prevent further incidents of crime and pauperism. It was even thought by some persons that a tax levied on each immigrant, to be expended by the common good of all, might tend to check immigration and to impoverish the immigrant. The general feeling became "the good of the country which receives the immigrant is quite as much to be considered as the good of the individual alien who, for one reason or another, comes to our shores. There was a time when convicts and the sweepings of London were shipped to Botany Bay. That was long ago but even now we receive a great many persons of the same class." *Report by F.B. Sanborn to the Commissioners of Public Charities and Corrections, 1876.*

Figure 3.4 This graphic picture shows how the Penitentiary was built into the side of a hill. Today the area is completely flat as a result of the heavy quarrying that removed most of the rock. (Photograph courtesy the Dan McDonough Collection)

Rather than call them prisons, penal reformers of the 19th century selected the term "penitentiary" using the time of confinement to help the inmates to become "penitent" for their crimes. To further mold them into productive citizens, work was provided to teach skills and a trade. Isolation was thought to be the best method of assisting the prisoner to become more penitent. Mixing of populations, the old and the young, the experienced and the first offender, allowed an exchange of mutual instructions on crime. There would be an opportunity to share stories, planning schemes, and the entire period of incarceration might become a school of crime. On the other hand, in a brief separate confinement, there was hope that a person charged with a first offense may realize his wrong doing and resolve to stop now and prevent a life of crime.

Figure 3.5 Looking north, the penitentiary is shown in the background. Next in line, coming toward the center of the picture stands the Gas Headquarters and the Electric Light Plant. To the right is another view of the hill that was quarried away. (Photograph courtesy the Dan McDonough Collection)

Communication between Snake Hill and the rest of Hudson County was limited. Letters could take up to a week to reach their destination. Sadly this was true in the case reported in this article written in *New York Tribune, August 2, 1916*:

## Child's Death Frees Father From Jail; End Came in Hospital Near Parent's Cell

Thomas Gambon of Bayonne, N.J. wound up a three-day celebration of his release from the Snake Hill jail at Bayonne Police Headquarters yesterday. Recorder Cain, learning that the man had just finished a year's sentence for habitual intoxication, sent him back to Snake Hill for another six months.

Gambon had hardly reached the prison when a breathless probation officer called for him with the news that he had been paroled. Not until he got home did Gambon learn the reason.

Three days before, his three year old son, Thomas Jr. had died from infantile paralysis in a hospital only a few yards from the jail at Snake Hill.

Figure 3.6 A lonely guard stands watch on Penitentiary Road. To the right are the beginnings of the vegetable garden and in back is the boat house. (Photograph courtesy the Dan McDonough Collection)

Presented are excerpts from another interesting newspaper article depicting harsh sentencing that often occurred. It appeared in *The Phillipsburg Mail, Phillipsburg, Montana, June 22, 1893*:

## After Eleven Years, Capture of an Escaped Convict Whose Supposed Dead Body Had Been Identified

The man in this case is William Cox a machinist who was convicted in January 1882, in Jersey City of stealing a watch and sentenced to a year's imprisonment in Snake Hill penitentiary. Cox declared his innocence, and his lawyer held out hopes of a pardon, but the prisoner got tired of waiting and escaped after serving five months of his sentence. Soon afterward a body was found in the Hackensack River and promptly identified as Cox. Nevertheless it wasn't his body they found. Cox was still alive, and 11 years to a day from the time of his escape, he was arrested by the same detective who had previously imprisoned him.

When Cox was once more imprisoned there and saw the futility of further concealment, he made a clean breast of the matters and told the following story of his escape:

"I was one of the quarry gang and soon saw there was only one place whence I could get possibly away. A big fellow called Joyce was keeper of the gang and of course armed with a rifle. At about 10 o'clock on May 9th Joyce ordered me to go half way up the hill to get a little blast ready.

I realized that this was chance and determined as I was walking up the hill that I would run for it if I had to die. Rather than live through those eight months of hell I would have been shot a hundred times over. I kept looking at Joyce out of the corner of my eye as I was going along. Just as I reached the hilltop I saw him turn his head around. I dropped into the underbrush, crawled like a snake along the ground until I gained the high timber; then I arose and ran for dear life toward the almshouse.

All at once I came upon two old men from the poorhouse sitting in the sun on the grass. They wore the pauper clothes, which are much like those that any poor fellow might wear. I had a quarter that I gave them and they turned me over a pair of overalls, a little check jumper and a cap. Then I felt ready for almost anything. I hurried to the edge of the woods and fell into an easy stride as I struck the road. I made to my wife's home in Brooklyn."

Cox said he went to work in Bridgeport the very next day and stayed there three months, after which he went to Philadelphia and then to England, whence he returned but a short time before he was re-arrested.

Between 1870 and 1873, statistical accounts were recorded for the crimes committed by criminals incarcerated in the Hudson County Penitentiary at Snake Hill. Among the charges which today may seem strange were: prize fighting, picking pockets, obstructing railroad, having burglar's tools, disorderly house, cutting timber, concealing pregnancy, concealing birth, and intent to ravish.

Figure 3.7 The New Jersey Trap Rock Company controlled the extensive stone quarry that was maintained on the western slope of the Hill. Van Winkle's *History of the Municipalities of Hudson County, New Jersey 1630-1923,* even stated "with stone crushers and other necessary equipment, operated under proper supervision by the inmates and of the institutions. Good road material is the result of their labor." (Photograph courtesy the Dan McDonough Collection)

The inmates participated in the work at the stone quarry, removing the trap rock which includes basalt. A major use for basalt is crushed rock for road and housing construction in concrete, macadam, and paving stones. Trap rock is also used as a ballast for railroad track bed. According to the 1909 map of Snake Hill, there was a six-acre quarry in the south western section of the Hill controlled by the New Jersey Trap Rock Company. Most of the rock was loaded onto barges at the water terminal.

In 1913, the United States Army Corps of Engineers conducted a study of water terminals and transfer facilities on rivers and harbors in the United States. This Report given to the War Department, included a section on the Hackensack River:

> The following docks located on the Hackensack River in the vicinity of Snake Hill whose privileges are extended to all on equal terms:
> - At Snake Hill, penitentiary dock, owned by the State of New Jersey
> - Jacob Schmitt's dock, Secaucus, New Jersey
> - River View Amusement Company dock, Secaucus, New Jersey, unavailable at low water
>
> The following of these docks have physical connection existing between them and the railroads serving the same territory: (Snake Hill and vicinity)
> - The New Jersey Trap Rock Company dock.
>
> The following dock located on the Hackensack River in the vicinity of Snake Hill, does not extend privileges of the dock to the public:
> - New Jersey Trap Rock Company dock, Snake Hill, New Jersey.
>
> In addition, this dock, and the penitentiary dock do not have approved and adequate highways leading directly to them and are approached indirectly through private roads.
>
> *Water Terminals and Transfer Facilities,*
> *Report of The Army Corps of Engineers, 1913.*

*Snake Hill Volume I*

Figure 3.8 The boat house is partially visible behind the vine-covered pagoda with its flag pole on top. In the distance is a large barn bordering the vast vegetable garden. (Photograph courtesy the Dan McDonough Collection)

The New Jersey Trap Rock Company employed men from neighboring towns in Hudson County. Most of them had a long walk to and from their homes. This becomes evident in following newspaper article from *The Evening World (New York, N.Y.), May 14, 1894*:

## Shot by Her Lover, Sadie Wertz Picked Up at Snake Hill

Another case of brutal assault was reported to Chief of Police Murphy this morning. Some workmen employed by the New Jersey Trap Rock Company at Snake Hill, while passing along an unfrequented road at 7:30 o'clock this morning on their way to work, discovered the body of a young woman lying near the Snake Hill Almshouse. The young woman was apparently about twenty-two years of age.

The workmen were shocked at the sight. The young woman was covered with blood that flowed from wounds in her head and body. She had been shot in the head and body.

The workmen listened at her heart to see if there was life remaining. There was a faint pulsation of the heart, which showed that she was not dead.

The workmen picked the young woman up and carried her into the Hudson County Almshouse at Snake Hill. She survived to press charges against her assailant.

Figure 3.9 The boat house rests proudly on the banks of the Hackensack River. The decorative flower garden was one of many that lined the roads at Snake Hill. (Photograph courtesy the Dan McDonough Collection)

Many of the crimes committed by those housed in the Penitentiary were theft and vagrancy as a result of seasonal unemployment and poverty. As mentioned, out-door relief, a form of welfare, was instituted to provide for immediate need. In New York City, nearly all who were given these payments were widows with families dependent on them. Very few males were furnished with out-door relief and only in extreme cases and during the inclement season, which if withheld would compel them to seek refuge in almshouses and become permanent paupers. It is in this view that relief is afforded, it served a benefit to city budgets, and at the same time offered help in time of need. "It is an evil that cannot be suppressed without causing them to become inmates of the almshouses, by which they and their children acquire habits of dependence, which grows with their growth, and is a greater injury to them, than the temporary receiving of alms." *Report of Out-Door Relief by Joshua Phillips to the Commissioners of Public Charities and Corrections, 1876.*

Figure 3.10 A view from the Hill, shows the Hackensack River winding its way northward. The penitentiary dock awaits the next barge to haul the quarried trap rock to its destination. (Photograph courtesy the Dan McDonough Collection)

The population of the Hudson County Penitentiary continued to grow at a remarkable pace. This, in part, was due to the inappropriate incarceration of some of the inmates. Petty crimes and unruly behavior in the Almshouse could be reason enough to have individuals locked up. The authorities knew that insanity was not a crime, and if the subject was not responsible for his acts, it was therefore an injustice to the "insane committer" of a crime to stigmatize him by the word *criminal* in connection with his *disease*. Therefore, if the person did not understand that he is guilty of a crime, imprisonment will not lead to repentance, only more frustration and confusion. The Freeholders of Hudson County once again realized the need for another institution to serve this completely different population. Plans began to construct a Lunatic Asylum at Snake Hill.

Figure 3.11 Rusted metal and broken pilings mark Snake Hill's once busy water bulkhead on the Hackensack River. In the distance stands an apartment complex in Secaucus. (Photograph from the author's private collection, April, 2013)

# Chapter Four

# The Lunatic Asylum

"What is insanity? Insanity is a disease of ignorance. The five leading factors are: wasteful living in various forms, overwork, inadequate funds, lack of ventilation, and neglect of moral culture. For the treatment of insane persons, as now administered in lunatic asylums for such unfortunates, the most that could be afforded is little more than a place where they may be isolated from society, kindly treated, and a watchful oversight maintained to prevent them from committing injury upon themselves or their attendants." *Paper by Nathan Allen M.D. to Fifth Annual Conference of Charities 1878.*

The paupers went to the almshouse, the criminals went to the penitentiary, and yet there was a population "hidden" among these two groups. People suffering with mental illness, referred to as lunatics, maniacs, or "the mad" were mixed in with both these, often referred to as the insane poor or the criminally insane. There was no appropriate place for them to receive care. It was realized that people deemed mad were crowding almshouses and prisons, and would be better served in a different kind of asylum.

The best form of provision for the care and control of the insane was in a place to keep them safe from themselves and others. This place of refuge was the lunatic asylum or madhouse as it was often called. Horror stories depict the use of chains, handcuffs, tranquilizer chairs, straitjackets, and filthy conditions in these institutions. This may have been true for some, but not for all lunatic asylums.

During the latter half of the 19th century, the New York and Philadelphia metropolitan areas experienced an increase in patients presenting mental illness. The question arose, was this increase due to an actual problem or was it because there was more awareness of the problem. Before the provision of lunatic asylums, those individuals with various degrees of mental illness were cared for at home, in almshouses, in hospitals, or even in prisons. One can only imagine the helplessness of someone suffering with a mental illness and having no visible means of support.

Prior to the construction of the Hudson County Lunatic Asylum at Snake Hill in 1873, many insane patients were subjected to various forms of mechanical restraint. They were place in small cells, and often deprived of the ordinary comforts of life. If the insane destroyed clothing, they were left without it; if they destroyed their furnishings, these were taken away; and if they refused to sleep on their beds, these too were removed.

The idea that lunacy could be prevented, presented itself in the mid-nineteenth century. Prior to this theory, the cause of insanity was obscure and mysterious, and was thought to be a possession by an evil spirit, so that it could not be fully understood, let alone cured. Most often the "evil" cause was referred to the church to contend with it. In comparison to the expenditure of funds and the efforts to cure the insane, no attempts were made to prevent it.

Caring for those who unfortunately cannot care for themselves has been the responsibility of the government. Public institutions faced a challenge to provide both a safe housing arrangement for the mentally ill and at the same time, attempt to provide a "cure" for their condition. Due to the lack of success, the number of the chronic insane continued to grow. In the New York Metropolitan area, lunatic asylums became crowded as the population grew and the illness became more recognizable and defined. Thus the management of such institutions became more and more burdensome.

It was in response to this growing need that in 1873, Hudson County built the Lunatic Asylum at Snake Hill. As with most public institutions, administration was handled by a county board who selected a superintendent who was in charge of the day-to-day operations.

Figure 4.1 Riding up the winding driveway after a long horse-drawn wagon ride from Jersey City, friends and family of prospective patients first saw the tall and looming buildings of the Lunatic Asylum at Snake Hill. (Photograph courtesy the Dan McDonough Collection)

Of all the buildings and services provided at Snake Hill, the one that carried the most stigma and shame was the Lunatic Asylum. Efforts were made to have the exterior of the institution nicely landscaped and favorable to visitors and patients alike. The classicism of the design displayed the benevolence for the insane and symbolized the order and discipline through which patients could be restored to reason. The challenge for the interior design was to balance a comfortable setting with tight security measures and adequate restraint for the patients; it needed to be as injury proof as possible. At the same time, the interior had to have good ventilation and convey a sense of order and healing with an atmosphere of cheerfulness and good taste. If a patient perceives upon admission, that the population is made up principally of patients who have been inmates for years and for whom there is no hope for a cure, the moral effect would have necessarily been depressing and disastrous upon the mind of such a patient and would have tended to retard his own recovery. The buildings of the Lunatic Asylum at Snake Hill were arranged with entrances facing the main road, the Administration Building was in the center, on one side was the Male Ward and on the other side was the Female Ward.

Figure 4.2 The 19th century Neoclassical French architectural design offered reassuring details and a therapeutic image that contributed to a sense of moral order for those who were to become a part of the institution. (Photograph courtesy the Dan McDonough Collection)

Early in the 19th century, the Quakers, who settled in Philadelphia and Boston, were opposed to the harsh treatment of the insane. They introduced an alternative form of care known as moral therapy. The Quakers believed that people who were suffering from madness should still be treated with kindness and gentle care. Moral therapy included shelter, good food and companionship. Even though the Quakers did not claim to know the origins of insanity, they felt that patients, above all, were still human beings and deserved to be treated like sane adults according to basic societal norms. Moral therapy would possibly help them get to a higher level of humanity while retaining their spiritual worth and inner harmony. This treatment proved to be successful until the lunatic asylums became overpopulated with inappropriate populations.

Defining someone as insane was a necessary prerequisite for being admitted to a facility. Following certification of insanity, the individual no longer had any rights.

In his *Paper presented to the National Conference on Social Welfare, 1874*, Dr. H. B. Wilbur wrote:

> Once committed to an asylum, for protection of society, real or supposed, they are kept in as positive confinement as if they were criminals. They are deprived of all control of person or property. They are placed under the charge of a physician and attendants, not of their own selection, and who are more than likely strangers to them.

Generally the laws in the later part of the 19th century relating to the committal of the insane in New Jersey required the certificate of one physician, under oath, setting forth two things: the insanity of the patient, and a recommendation for placement of some kind if necessary. This certificate was to be sworn to before, and approved by, a judge of the state and county where this person resided. This sworn testimony was required from a "respectable physician" and neither the courts nor the law made much discrimination in the qualifications or the character of the physician. It was easy to find such physicians everywhere. The problem came not so much from bribery or any self-interest, as from the fact that these certificates were too quickly signed, without careful examination. It was quite a responsibility for the physician to swear an oath and commit the individual to a lunatic asylum.

When compared with criminal proceedings, the law stipulated that the vagrant and the criminal could not be punished without a trial by a judge or jury, and afforded counsel who presented a set of evidence and facts. There were greater safeguards and defenses for the criminal than were provided to protect the insane.

Even though a person was declared insane, he might not be a candidate for a lunatic asylum. The principles that governed commitment included the common law right of confining the insane who were dangerous to be at large, or to secure them for proper treatment. It was recognized that even though people were deemed "insane" they were still good citizens and with the help of friends and family could remain in their community. For these individuals it would have been an injustice to remove them to a custodial institution. Therefore it was important that the certificate for commitment not only contain the declaration of insanity but also the explicit recommendation for confinement for good and sufficient reasons. Reasons for confinement included the harmless insane who required custody for their own protection and comfort. Perhaps they were neglected and mistreated at home, or others who wandered about and were homeless.

In addition, violence and a danger to themselves often were reasons for seeking commitment, sometimes behavior was simply so destructive that the family could no longer tolerate his or her presence in the household. In the mid-nineteenth century it was unusual for families to commit relatives on the grounds that they may be cured or be more comfortable in the asylum.

The following article relates a common method of commitment. It was published in the *New-York Tribune (New York, N.Y.) April 7, 1883:*

## Mr. Martin Declared Insane

A commission appointed yesterday, to investigate the mental condition of John Martin, of Jersey City, declared him insane. Martin was hurt by a collision at the Pennsylvania Ferry in February, 1881, his injuries resulting in insanity. Dr. George W. King, superintendent of the Lunatic Asylum, testified that Martin was taken to that institution in December 1882, suffering from religious mania. The patient declared that he had seen God, and had shaken hands with Him, and that God had commissioned him to go to Snake Hill and reform the county institutions there. He also asserted himself the owner of the Pennsylvania Railroad and the greater portion of Jersey City. The doctor was of the opinion that Martin was mentally unfit to transact business. Martin's wife testified that he had threatened her life at one time, saying God had instructed him to kill her and marry some younger woman.

Martin was called to the stand, and made a statement in an apparently rational manner. He said that God had never spoken to him except in a dream, and had told him to lead a better life. On being asked why he had been sent to the asylum, he said he did not know, unless it was a trick of his lawyer to secure heavy damages from the Pennsylvania Railroad Company in a suit which was then pending. He believed the trick was successful, because he got a verdict of $20,000. At the conclusion of the investigation Martin was taken back to the asylum.

Figure 4.3 Male and female patients had entirely separate departments. Within each department, each ward had its own staircase, so that patients could go to a lounge such as the one pictured here, without walking through another ward. (Photograph courtesy the Dan McDonough Collection)

Unlike other hospitals in which patients were treated for various ailments, broken bones, and then released, the patients in lunatic asylums tended to stay for longer periods of time. The numbers kept increasing, causing the need for more custodial care rather than treatment. Care for the insane was experimental at best, often modeling treatment modalities used in Europe. Using a holistic model "a sound mind in a sound body," treatment consisted of daily exercise, strict routine, and outdoor activities. Patients were taken outside to get fresh air and sunshine during the day. In the bad weather, they would be given occupational therapy consisting of arts and crafts, or even helping with some chores on the farm. Overcrowding caused asylums to turn into custodial institutions; as soon as they opened they became filled with a class of cases, three-fourths of whom were chronic and hopelessly insane patients, very few of whom could ever have benefited by curative treatment. They no longer needed the same medical skill and large number of attendants that were provided in hospitals. They simply required a place to live and were given their basic needs. However, even though they were not hospitals, these receptacles for the retention of patients were at a great cost. In addition, the asylums suffered from overcrowding and poor ventilation.

Men and women were housed in separate buildings on either side of the Administration Building. Ward assignments were based on the patient's level of manageability and the probability of violent acts; and filthy habits. For placement purposes, the insane were divided into several categories: the imbecile; the maniac; the furious maniac; the idiot; the lunatic; and being mad. Each category was described with a list of "evil" causes that included pauperism, feebleness, sensual disorder, and social misconduct such as drunkenness and masturbation.

The best behaved patients lived on the upper floors, along with quiet, chronic patients. The violent and destructive ones were placed on the lower floors, but away from the administration building because of their noise and odors. Each floor had its own hall to the dining room and sitting rooms so the patients did not have to travel through a ward to reach them.

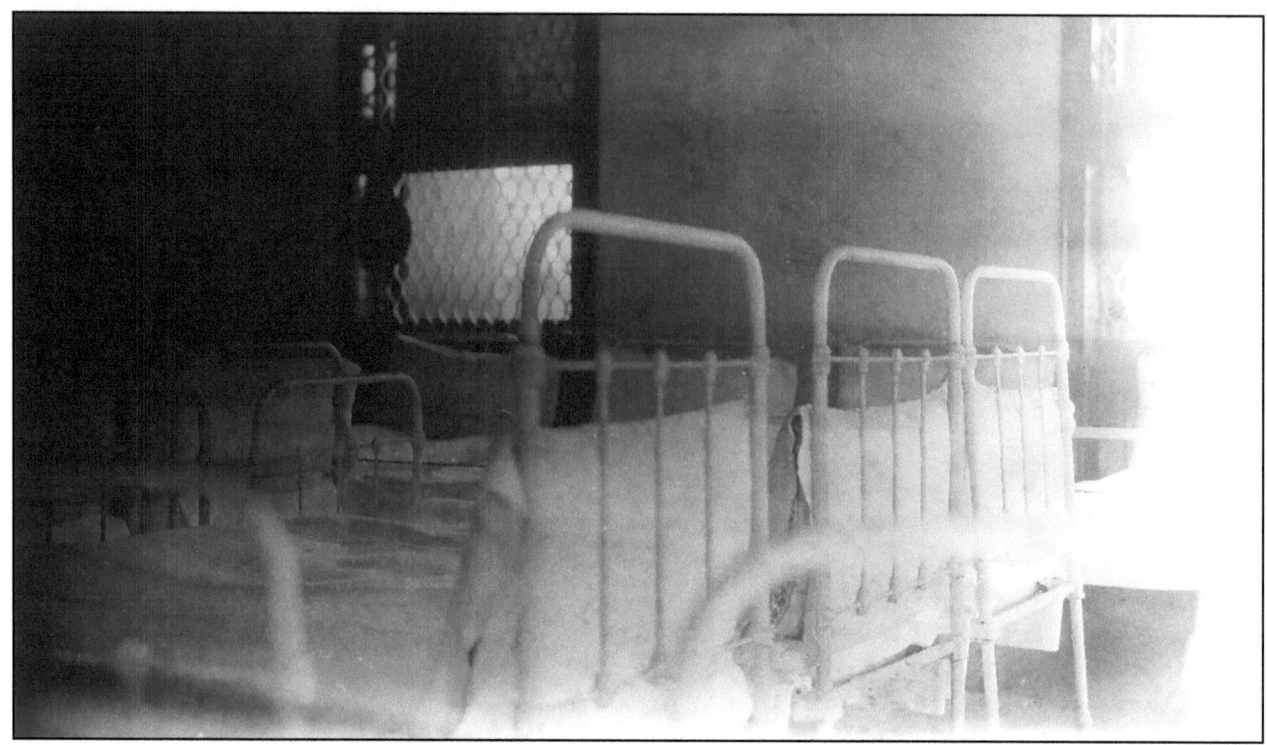

Figure 4.4 There were window gratings to provide maximum security. These beds were probably being stored for future use. (Photograph courtesy the Dan McDonough Collection)

Mental Health advocates had a dramatic impact on services in the New York metropolitan area. Perhaps the most significant advocate was Dorothea Dix. As an avid reformer she urged state governments to provide care and treatment for the insane poor. She admired the Quaker view of moral treatment, and advocated kindness and the beauty of natural surroundings. She believed many patients should be engaged in outdoor work, gardening, farming, which brings them outdoors into the pure fresh air. It is of great value to the patients, by promoting digestion and strengthening the muscular system. Light work gives the patient something to think about and occupies his mind in a healthful manner. In fact most successful lunatic asylums were located on large farms.

Much of her time was spent visiting almshouses, prisons, and lunatic asylums and writing the results of her investigations. Becoming an authority on asylum architecture, Dorothea Dix was asked to help design the New Jersey State Lunatic Asylum at Trenton in 1848.

Her work took her to New York, New Jersey, Pennsylvania, and Illinois, and helped reform major prisons and insane asylums. In addition she served as director of Civil War army nurses. In 1881 the legislature of New Jersey voted to provide a retirement home for her within Trenton Psychiatric Hospital. She lived there until her death in 1887.

Figure 4.5 Panoramic view of the Lunatic Asylum at Snake Hill. Note the letters indicating "HCIH" for Hudson County Insane Hospital in front. (Photograph courtesy the Dan McDonough Collection)

Another advocate for asylum reform was Nellie Bly. In 1887, as a reporter for the *New York World,* Nellie was given the assignment to explore the conditions of insane asylums in the New York metropolitan area. She selected the Lunatic Asylum on Blackwell Island in New York City. After pretending to be insane, she convinced authorities and was committed to Blackwell Island. Her mission was simple. She was to describe the conditions, and objectively report them, both good and bad. For Nellie, it was an opportunity to learn firsthand how the insane were cared for and the conditions that existed in an insane asylum. When she asked how she would get out, her editor was not quite sure, but he guaranteed they would get her out. Under the name of Nellie Brown, she spent ten days there until her discharge through the efforts of her editor. She wrote an expose of her experiences and as a result, many reforms were instituted at Blackwell Island as well as more state funding to continue to improve conditions at all New York Lunatic Asylums.

Nellie Bly's concerns about "getting out" of the Lunatic Asylum on Blackwell Island leads to the overall question of the conditions of discharge. Henry Hurd, Editor, *The Institutional Care of the Insane in the United States and Canada, 1916*, mentions that conditions of discharge in New Jersey were "On certificate of complete recovery from the director of the hospital, the managers may discharge any patients except those under criminal charges. They may also discharge unrecovered patients or return them to the almshouse of the county. No provision exists for parole."

Even when conditions inside the lunatic asylums improved, successful "treatment" did not necessarily follow. As a result, the number of chronic insane continued to grow. In the New York metropolitan area, lunatic asylums became crowded as the population grew, and as insanity became more recognizable and defined.

Figure 4.6 More buildings were built to meet the demand for services as the population of chronic insane patients increased at Snake Hill. (Photograph courtesy the Dan McDonough Collection)

In New Jersey a number of county institutions, similar to the Lunatic Asylum at Snake Hill, sprang up because of the overcrowding at the state hospitals and the continued inability for chronic patients to remain in their homes. Smaller buildings were added to accommodate the chronic insane, farm laborers, and harmless persons requiring custodial care rather than stricter institutional treatment. County officials were encouraged by the State to care for their own residents. Whenever possible, patients were returned from State hospitals to their county of origin as described in the following article: *The sun (New York, N.Y.) May 15, 1896:*

## Hudson County Insane Go to Snake Hill

Morristown, May 14.-The two hundred Hudson County inmates of the State Hospital for the Insane at Morris Plains were transferred today to the Hudson County Insane Asylum at Snake Hill. While dinner was being served a special train of four passenger coaches arrived upon the hospital grounds. It was in charge of Dr. King, warden of the Hudson County institution with a corps of attendants. The inmates then embarked upon the waiting cars. The majority of the patients regarded the trip as an excursion, and were as jolly and happy as a party of school children. The train reached Snake Hill over the Boonton branch and main line of the Delaware, Lackawanna and Western Railroad in time for supper. The departure of this large number of inmates will greatly relieve the overcrowded condition of the hospital.

Doctors used a very broad approach to diagnostic categories that required institutionalization. So little was known about insanity and those having to make a diagnosis were most often basing their conclusions upon observation and family reports. Sometimes it was an extreme change in characteristic behavior: the quiet became noisy; the loud became withdrawn; the industrious had given up work; and the agnostics became religious fanatics. But whatever the diagnosis given to them, the treatment of the patient upon admission depended on their manageability and their ability to live peacefully in the ward. An extreme attempt for a cure is detailed in the following article from the *Spokane Press, (Spokane, Wash.) August 8, 1908*:

## Surgical Aid to Altar Character

NEW YORK, Aug, 8-With the hope of changing the character of her daughter that she may be able to distinguish right from wrong, Mrs. Margaret Brennan of Long Island city desires to have a surgical operation performed and the evil portion of her daughter's brain removed.

The young woman is Mrs. Paul Kelly and she is presently serving a six-month sentence in the Snake Hill reformatory on the charge of petty thievery.

The mother claims that her daughter was led astray by a foreign servant girl, who came to live with the family when the child was only 7 years old. The maid taught the child to steal.

Figure 4.7 Hallway with patients' rooms, probably at the Male Department. At the far end, figures can be seen in a small lounge. (Photograph courtesy the Dan McDonough Collection)

At Snake Hill, administrators were challenged with the task of providing a pleasant atmosphere for patients and their visitors, and at the same time, implementing strict security measures to prevent violent outbreaks and suicide attempts. Extensive padding and window gratings were evident in the wards and sitting areas.

Figure 4.8 Patients from the Women's Department at dinner. Every detail from the serving to the table settings in the wards was meant to sustain the impression that here was an institution where patients received competent care. (Photograph courtesy the Dan McDonough Collection)

In many asylums an incentive system was implemented. As a way to control behavior, a system of rewards and punishments manipulated ward assignments. If the patient was behaved and orderly, they would move to wards with similar manageable patients. If they became violent or indulged in filthy habits, they were moved to separate, more restrictive wards. In addition, such privileges as going to the lounge or recreation activities were removed.

Figure 4.9 Large windows and rooms that were airy with high ceilings presented a healing interior. Security measures were always in place, window gratings and padding on the bench and support column. The furniture was designed to have no sharp corners, no projections, and as injury-proof as possible. (Photograph courtesy the Dan McDonough Collection)

Security and dignity while in confinement required a delicate balance. Patients in the Lunatic Asylum at Snake Hill were removed from a position of independence and freedom to one of confinement. But that was not all, the moral effect, the stigma carried with it a sense of degradation and humiliation. Unfortunately, in a large number of cases, the stigma carried with mental illness still exists today.

Figure 4.10 The wards were secure, some with guards to protect the more violent patients from themselves and others. In post-Civil War years, house staff, as shown in this photograph, were issued military-style uniforms expressing authority and responsibility. Note the fire hose station at the top of the stairway. (Photograph courtesy the Dan McDonough Collection)

Figure 4.11 Pictured is an original, early antique, gilt metal button worn on staff uniforms at the Hudson County Lunatic Asylum during the late 1800's. (Button is from the author's private collection)

# Chapter Five

# The Infectious Disease Hospitals

"There is perhaps no greater charity than that of giving a hopelessly ill man or woman a comfortable bed to die in; and in very many intermediate cases, while recovery cannot be hoped for, much may be done by medical skill and kind care, to prolong life and alleviate suffering. *Annual Report, 1880,* Episcopal Hospital, Philadelphia, PA.

Hospitals in the last half of the 19th century were not a welcome place for the sick. No one wanted to have a loved one, or even a servant leave home and be cared for by strangers. As a result, it was the very sick, dependent, and diseased who were treated in hospitals. Because friends and family waited until the sick person reached a critical state, by the time they were finally admitted, a large percentage died while at the hospital. Therefore, the negative feeling that "people who go into the hospital never come home again," prevailed. It became more and more evident that the mid-nineteenth century hospital was no more than a place where the poor went to die. As the municipal institutions became burdened with large proportions of chronic and incurable cases, the result was higher and higher death rates.

With the continued spread of such infectious diseases as smallpox and tuberculosis, local governments realized that these patients could no longer be placed in the same institutions as other patients. Private hospitals began turning these cases away and Health Officials in Hudson County, facing a further spread of disease, refused to let those infected remain in their homes. There was a similar experience happening at Snake Hill. Those paupers falling ill with smallpox increased fears of the spread of the disease to patients in the Lunatic Asylum and the inmates of the Almshouse. Prisoners in the Penitentiary were also at risk. After the completion of the Almshouse in 1863, the Penitentiary in 1870, and the Lunatic Asylum in 1873, Hudson County built several infectious disease hospitals. These included a Smallpox Hospital, an Isolation Hospital, and several Tuberculosis Hospitals and Pavilions.

Fear of further spread of smallpox was reported in this article from *New-York Tribune (New York, N.Y.) March 23, 1893.*

## News from New Jersey - Small Pox at Snake Hill

For several months smallpox has been prevalent in Hudson County. The patients were sent to the pest house at Snake Hill. As a result, the hospital was overcrowded, and tents were erected, mainly however, for the use of convalescents. Owing to a lack of nurses, these were not looked after as closely as they should have been, and were allowed to mingle with aged male paupers, who were kept in what is called the "old men's pavilion." As a result, smallpox has broken out in the pavilion, and there is danger that the disease may spread to the penitentiary and the lunatic and orphan asylums.

Hereafter the men will be under quarantine, as will be all the institutions, and there will be no communication between Snake Hill and the outside world, except under medical inspection, until the danger is over.

Figure 5.1 Steep steps lead to the Administration Building of the Tuberculosis Department at Snake Hill. (Photograph courtesy the Dan McDonough Collection)

Of all the patients treated for infectious diseases at Snake Hill, those suffering from tuberculosis and smallpox were among the highest in number. Tuberculosis is a disease that typically attacks the lungs, but can also affect other parts of the body. It is spread through the air when people who have an active tuberculosis infection cough or sneeze. In the 19th century, tuberculosis caused widespread public concern and was considered a disease of the urban poor. After it was determined to be contagious, those who contracted the disease needed to be isolated. The rationale for isolation in a special hospital was that a regimen of rest and good nutrition offered the best chance of recovery. Patients were exposed to plentiful amounts of high altitude, fresh air, and good nutrition.

Figure 5.2 A two-story Tuberculosis Infirmary is pictured with patients sitting in the fresh air. Behind to the left is the Almshouse. Up the hill to the left is the Caroline B. Alexander Pavilion for Tuberculosis patients. (Photograph courtesy the Dan McDonough Collection)

Although Robert Koch discovered the identifying specific causative agents of tuberculosis, cholera, and anthrax and thus gave experimental support for the concept of infectious disease, how to control the spread of these diseases and how to treat them were still in the experimental stages.

Ideas about the nature of disease and its transmission were passed down and along with it the social attitudes, rather than the scientific facts. Subsequently, these attitudes were reflected in the organization of the hospital. For example, fresh air was thought necessary to keep the body in a balanced state. Most importantly, as the majority of mid-century clinicians would have conceded, there were no substitutes for rest, a nourishing diet, warmth, cleanliness, and good nursing.

Figure 5.3 A closer view of the Tuberculosis Infirmary shows the front porch and an attendant with patients outside in the sunshine. A large amount of fresh air was an important part of their treatment. (Photograph courtesy the Dan McDonough Collection)

Large city hospitals were located in the heart of the busy and crowded industrial areas. Often it was a matter of life or death for workplace accident victims who suffered some sort of trauma on the job to get to a hospital as quickly as possible. Traveling a great distance by horse and wagon could cost a life. These hospitals were several stories high to provide care for as many as possible. However, by the 19th century the increase in infectious disease cases caused a change to hospital architecture.

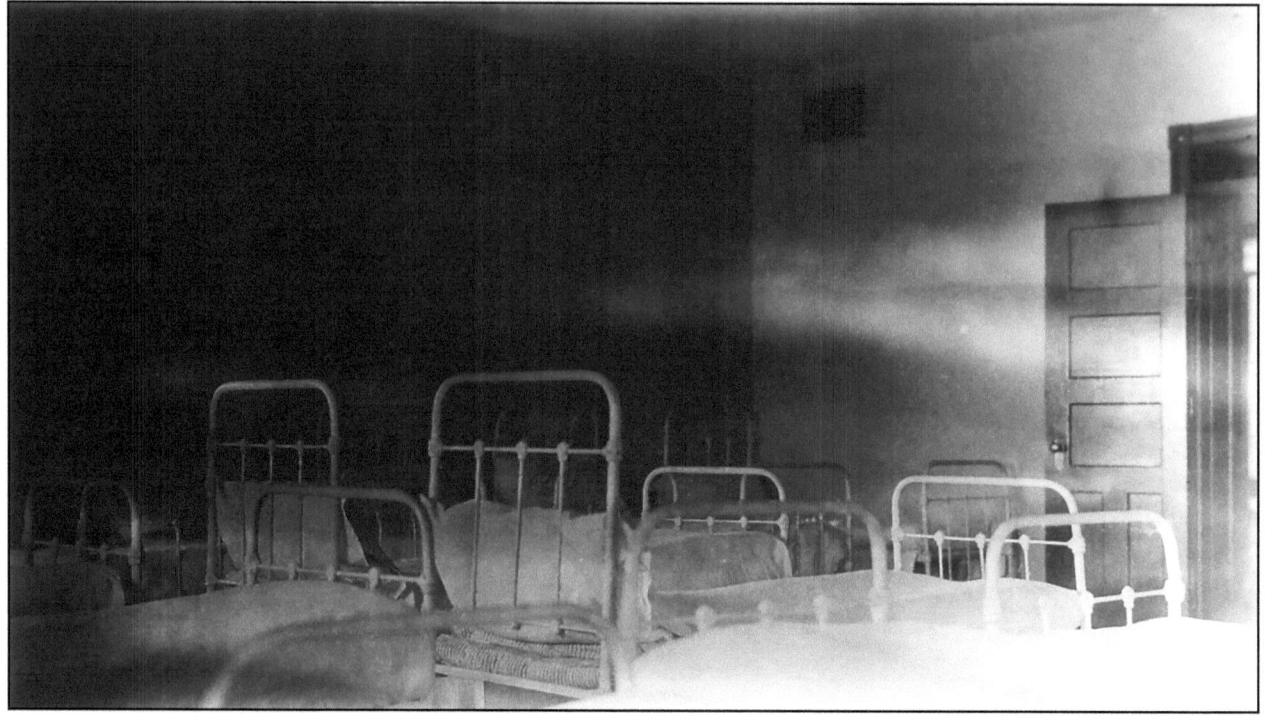

Figure 5.4 Beds crowded in a room during fumigation and scouring of a ward that was contaminated. During an outbreak of an infectious disease, the infected ward was "aired" to remove disease-inducing materials, and the contaminated materials were burned in the incinerator. (Photograph courtesy the Dan McDonough Collection)

The pavilion hospital was found to maximize the circulation of air and sanitary conditions. The pavilion plan specified wards ventilated by large and numerous windows on both long sides with doors at each end. The goal was to maximize ventilation and limit crowding. Pavilion design also implied low, one or two-story sprawling clinics as opposed to the higher and denser hospitals in congested urban areas. In warm weather, a tent could temporarily substitute as a hospital setting to provide excellent ventilation and prove more healthful than larger institutions. During the summer months at Snake Hill, tents were used for some patients with tuberculosis.

Figure 5.5 The Caroline B. Alexander Pavilion was an example of the architectural design that allowed the most fresh air and ventilation for tuberculosis patients. The pavilion was named for Mrs. Alexander who was a leader in social work and charities in the New York metropolitan area. Note the church steeple behind the pavilion. (Photograph courtesy the Dan McDonough Collection)

One of the tuberculosis pavilions on the Hill was named in honor of Caroline B. Alexander. She was among the most notable social workers in Hudson County and a prominent citizen of Hoboken. Mrs. Alexander devoted her time to sociological and philanthropic work in New Jersey and New York. She served as President of the New Jersey State Board of Children's Guardians, and was a member of the Women's Reformatory Commission. In addition she was a founding member of the New Jersey State Charity Aid Association. Mrs. Alexander was the oldest daughter of Col. Edwin Stevens, whose family has an extensive lineage in Hoboken, and helped found such institutions as Stevens Institute of Technology, and Church of the Holy Innocents, an Episcopalian Church.

Figure 5.6 Climbing up the hillside, similar fresh air pavilions were positioned to maximize proper ventilation. The more serious patients were treated in these pavilions; even tents were used in warmer weather. (Photograph courtesy the Dan McDonough Collection)

The Caroline B. Alexander Pavilion was one of several pavilions that housed tuberculosis patients. These were placed along the side of the Hill. The more acute cases were in these higher pavilions to give them more fresh air. It was believed that sickness was a result of an imbalance of diet, poor ventilation, or inactivity. Therefore "treatment" centered upon returning the body to its proper balance by good food, proper ventilation, exercise and activity. Medicines were limited since physicians could not easily accept the idea that a specific substance could prevent or cure a specific ailment. Drugs were administered to adjust the body's internal balance.

Medicine could not be counted on for a cure, in fact, it sometimes was given with the understanding that death was inevitable, but the patient would benefit from some sort of relief until the end came. The natural course of some ills was toward death.

Perhaps one of the more important distinctions to note regarding contagious disease, was that it crossed all social boundaries. As a result, the infectious disease hospitals at Snake Hill would have patients who were in the upper and middle social classes as well as the poor. When someone fell ill to a contagious disease such as smallpox and could not arrange to go to a private hospital, the Health Inspectors in the County had to send them to Snake Hill to control the outbreak.

In an effort to control an outbreak of smallpox, government teamed with health officials to find a solution. This article relates how different departments in Hudson County cooperated in an effort to stop the spread of the infection. *Evening Star (Washington, D.C.), December 19, 1874:*

## Smallpox in Jersey City

In spite of the precautions adopted by the Board of Health of Hudson County, N.J., to prevent the spread of smallpox, that dreaded malady is on the increase. A hospital has been erected specially for such patients on the county grounds at Snake Hill, and ambulances are being constructed under the direction of the Board of Freeholders. Four weeks ago there were just half a dozen patients, yesterday there were twenty. The number of fatal cases during the month of November was six. The disease has been so virulent that only five per cent of the patients have recovered. Between the board of freeholders and the physicians composing the board of health the construction of county ambulances has been delayed. The freeholders at their meeting yesterday, spent over half an hour in discussing the question whether the driver of the ambulance should live at the hospital and what would be the chances of the horse in escaping the disease.

Hudson County built ambulances specifically for the transport of smallpox patients. To help contain the contagion, the driver of the ambulance was housed at Snake Hill. The lack of knowledge and the fear of contagion went as far as concern for the horses that pulled the smallpox ambulances.

Figure 5.6A Pictured is a horse-drawn ambulance from Bellevue Hospital, New York City. Hudson County used similar ambulances exclusively to transport smallpox patients to Snake Hill. (Image courtesy of The Lillian and Clarence de la Chapelle Medical Archives at New York University)

Because of the fear of an epidemic and the lack of knowledge regarding the cause and control of the contagion, most of the bodies of those who died of their disease were buried at Snake Hill rather than transported by special ambulance for funeral and burial in their home community.

Normally a body would be transported in a covered funeral wagon. In the 19$^{th}$ century, most funerals were privately held in the home. If someone had a loved one who died of an infectious disease while at Snake Hill, it was not very likely that they would have the body transported back home for a viewing and funeral. Most probably they would have had them buried in one of the burial grounds at Snake Hill.

Another reference to the smallpox ambulance comes from an article in the *New-York Tribune (New York, N.Y. July 23, 1888.*

## News from the Suburbs – Jersey City

Charles Richter, age fourteen, of Hoboken was attacked with smallpox thirteen days ago, and notice was sent to the county authorities a few days later. The smallpox ambulance from the hospital at Snake Hill was sent to the house yesterday to remove the patient, but his mother objected to his removal because he was out of danger and nearly convalescent. Dr. Herzog was called in and advised the boy's removal, and he was taken away despite his mother's protest.

The medical belief was that the central mode of causation of infection was the atmosphere; the more crowded and poorly ventilated a building, the greater the danger to its patients. The larger number of persons with the disease in a crowded space, the greater the contamination of the air they breathed. The following article from *The evening world. (New York, N.Y.), February 21, 1893* describes how quickly smallpox spread in the Jersey City tenement houses:

## Small-Pox Nest in Jersey

Seven cases of small-pox in one home. That is the latest discovery made by a Jersey City Health Inspector.
About two weeks ago Lizzie Stumpf, aged eight, was taken sick at her home in the big double tenement-house on Coles Street in Jersey City, Her parents thought she had a mild attack of measles, and did not think it necessary to call a physician.
Under home treatment the child was progressing well, and not until yesterday was it even surmised that she was afflicted with small-pox.
Last evening six members of the family of Mrs. Meade, who occupies the top floor and keeps borders, were taken sick, and a physician called, who at once pronounced the disease with which all six were afflicted to be small-pox. Then it was made known for the first time that the Stumpf child had the disease.
The Health Inspector was notified and the six new cases immediately removed to the small-pox hospital at Snake Hill.

Figure 5.7 Rising above the salt marsh, the buildings of the Lunatic Asylum stand in the front and behind are the Administration Building of the Tuberculosis Department, the Pavilions and the churches. (Photograph courtesy the Dan McDonough Collection)

The three best preventive measures were considered to be: avoid overcrowding, enforce cleanliness, and promote ventilation. Buildings were constructed not only in the appropriate style of architecture but also for their peculiar fitness for the purpose for which they were designed. Therefore with respect to infectious disease hospitals, special attention was given to not only sanitation but also to the proper air space for wards. Through the system of ventilation adopted, fresh pure air was continually admitted as the impure air was expelled. The smaller pavilions avoided overcrowding by reducing the number of beds in each ward. In addition, metal instead of wooden bed frames helped minimize the accumulation of dirt and germs.

Figure 5.8 Pictured is a dirt road leading to the Isolation Hospital for patients with such contagious diseases such as Typhoid Fever and Diphtheria. There was also a Smallpox Hospital at Snake Hill. (Photograph courtesy the Dan McDonough Collection)

Hospital construction during this period emphasized the placement of windows and doors to maximize the circulation of fresh air. In fact, the well-planned hospital was carefully located in a site that was preferably far from the city's congested areas, and near open fields. Ideally it would also be located near a river or body of water with fresh breezes to replace the hospital's tainted air. The higher the pavilions were placed on Snake Hill, the closer they met this ideal criteria. This guideline was also practiced in Philadelphia and New York when selecting sites for their hospitals and almshouses. Most had riverside locations.

Figure 5.9 An important part of controlling an outbreak of infectious disease was burning the contaminated materials. An incinerator was used to dispose of many infected items, as well as waste from the other buildings. (Photograph courtesy the Dan McDonough Collection)

After an outbreak of an infectious disease, patients had to be removed to isolated wards or rooms, the contaminated ward was fumigated and scoured and the bedding burned. The room was thoroughly aired to remove disease-causing materials that remained in the atmosphere.

Figure 5.10 Burning contaminated materials in an incinerator such as the one pictured, was as close to disease control as health professionals could come to understand in the 19$^{th}$ century. Germ theory was not fully endorsed, and many followed the guidelines of cleanliness and good ventilation as the best form of treatment. (Photograph courtesy the Dan McDonough Collection)

Figure 5.11 A lonely, crumbling smoke stack is a remaining monument, standing tribute to the facility that served Hudson County for more than a hundred years. (Photograph from the author's private collection, April 2013)

# Chapter Six

# The Look Homeward

Figure 6.1 Looking homeward from "The Hill" down the long road, one can see images of people walking home after visiting loved ones or returning from work, sharing the road with an occasional horse-drawn bakery wagon or ambulance This stretch of road winding through the salt marsh connected the patients at Snake Hill with other parts of Hudson County and their homes. (Photograph courtesy the Dan McDonough Collection)

Reviewing all the different populations who arrived at the Hill, and the many services provided for their care, one of the first questions most would ask would be "Who went to Snake Hill?" From newspaper reports and a review of society during the end of the 19th century the answer would include: the poor and homeless, the chronically ill, the insane, the elderly, and criminals. In addition, there were those who did not fit any of these categories, but had no family to care for them, could not speak English, or found themselves too depressed and downtrodden to continue life without help. Perhaps the family caring for their loved could no longer endure the problematic behavior, or became too old to continue adequate care.

What happened at Willard Asylum for the Chronic Insane in New York State could be compared to what happened at the Lunatic Asylum at Snake Hill. Willard opened its doors in1869, about the same time as the asylum at Snake Hill. Willard was the final home for many who went there. When they arrived, their bags were stored, and most never reclaimed for the trip home. What was in the bags? Who helped pack them, and what were their thoughts as they packed the bags? After Willard closed in 1995, over 400 of these bags were found and the contents preserved. Stories remain to be told. Most probably the stories depicted in the Willard suitcases are similar to the stories of those who went to Snake Hill.

Figure 6.2 Anna's suitcase, one of the 82 Willard suitcases poignantly photographed by Jon Crispin. Anna was a patient at Willard Psychiatric Center in upstate New York. Her suitcase was among the more than 400 found in the hospital attic after Willard closed in 1995. (Photograph courtesy of Jon Crispin, Photographer)

Similarly to what happened at Willard, after a person was admitted to Snake Hill, their families experienced difficulty in travel, and perhaps the fear of contagion. Subsequently the visits became less and less until not at all. The importance of finding such relics as the suitcases is that here are over 400 stories to tell. One wonders about the other stories; the ones that will forever remain untold.

Figure 6.3 Eleanor's suitcase reveals a great deal about her life at the time she packed her things and went to Willard. The contents portray her as a woman who was both sophisticated and socially astute. She included her packing list: *shirts, slips, night dress, handkerchiefs, and waistcoat*. Her bottle of perfume, Isabey of 20 rue de la Paix, was imported from Paris, France. She enjoyed sewing and packed her sewing kit, complete with needles, buttons, and a needle threader. Included were two patterns: McCall's Ladies' Dress pattern 6802, and one for elegant crocheted gloves. Reading material included an article from *Country Gentleman*, offering guidelines for winter entertaining. Sadly, Eleanor never returned home to fulfill her dreams of wearing beautiful dresses and being the perfect hostess. Like so many who entered the mental asylums at the turn of the century, she too never went home again. (Photograph courtesy of Jon Crispin, Photographer)

During the 19th and 20th centuries, across the United States, hundreds of thousands of state and county hospital patients were buried in anonymously numbered graves. It was often said that these patients' remains were treated with the same lack of recognition and dignity that was their lot while they lived.

After someone died at Snake Hill, be they patients of the hospitals, the inmates of the almshouses or the penitentiary, the next of kin was notified to arrange for burial. In situations when no one claimed the body, it was buried in one of the burial grounds. Bodies were buried two in a grave, one on top of another. They were marked with a numbered cast-iron grave marker in lieu of a gravestone. So many dependent souls whose situation in life brought them to "the Hill," and perhaps spent decades there, died away from their homes. Most were buried on the grounds, and marked with a number instead of a name.

Today the buildings have disappeared, many of the burial grounds are unmarked and forgotten, and even the land has largely been obliterated by quarrying, yet Snake Hill still has a story to tell. Volume Two of this series attempts to answer some of the more puzzling questions: Why did the buildings disappear? What happened to the burial grounds? and perhaps most importantly, Why do these mysteries of Snake Hill and its ghosts continue to haunt us?

Figure 6.4 The view from the top of the Hill looking east, shows the Tuberculosis pavilions, the tops of the churches and the Almshouse. Snake Hill was home to a community that comprised many different populations, all in need of help and all living and working together to survive. (Photograph courtesy the Dan McDonough Collection)

Figure 6.5 Today, the view from Snake Hill shows the skyline of Manhattan fifteen minutes away. Millions travel through the Lincoln Tunnel, take the New Jersey Turnpike to Newark Airport and other points south, never realizing that drive past Snake Hill and its lasting mysteries. (Photograph courtesy of Andy Kazmierski, Photographer. April 2012)

# References

American Medico-Psychological Association, New York (State). State Lunatic Asylum, Anonymous. *The American Journal of Insanity, Volume 3. 1846.*

Ackerknecht, Erwin H. *A Short History of Medicine.* Baltimore: The Johns Hopkins University Press, 1982.

Beard, Mary Ritter. *Woman's Work in Municipalities.* New York: D. Appleton and Company, 1915.

Bly, Nellie. *Ten Days in a Mad-House.* Printed in United States, 1887.

Breckinridge, Henry. *Water Terminal and Transfer Facilities*, Letter from the Acting Secretary of War. U.S. Army Corps of Engineers. 1913.

Gamwell, Lynn & Tomes, Nancy. *Madness in American: Cultural and Medical Perceptions of Mental Illness before 1914.* Ithaca, NY: Cornell University Press, 1995.

Gollaher, David. *Voice for the Mad, The Life of Dorothea Dix.* New York: The Free Press, 1995.

Hurd, Henry M. et al. *The Institutional Care of the Insane in the United States and Canada.* Baltimore: The Johns Hopkins Press, 1916.

Irving, Washington. *Knickerbocker's History of New York, Complete.* Chicago: W. B. Conkey Company, 1824. reprint 2013.

Johnston, Norman. *Eastern State Penitentiary, Crucible of Good Intentions.* U.S.: Department of Publications and Graphics, 1994.

Lawrence, Charles. *History of the Philadelphia almshouses and hospitals: from the beginning of the eighteenth century to the ending of the nineteenth centuries.* Published by Charles Lawrence, 1905.

Levenson, Dorothy. *Montefiore, The Hospital as Social Instrument.* New York: Farrar, Straus & Giroux, 1984.

Lightner, David. L. *Asylum, Prison, and Poorhouse, The Writings and Reform Work of Dorothea Dix in Illinois.* Carbondale: Southern Illinois University Press, 1999.

Macy, Sue. *Bylines, A Photobiography of Nellie Bly.* Washington, D.C.: National Geographic, 2009.

Penney, Darby & Stastny, Peter. *The Lives They Left Behind.* New York: Bellevue Literary Press, 2008.

Rieser, Robert. Editor. *History of Hudson County and of the Old Village of Bergen.* Jersey City: Trust Company of New Jersey, 1921.

Riis, Jacob A. *The Children of The Poor.* New York: Charles Scribner's Sons, 1892.

Rosenberg, Charles E. *The Care of Strangers, The Rise of America's Hospital System.* Baltimore: The Johns Hopkins University Press, 1987.

Tomes, Nancy. *A generous confidence Thomas Story Kirkbride and the art of asylum-keeping, 1840-1883.* Cambridge: Cambridge University Press, 1984.

Van Winkle, Daniel. *History of the Municipalities of Hudson County, New Jersey 1630-1923.* New York: Lewis Historical Publishing Company, 1924.

Winfield, Charles H. *History of the County of Hudson, New Jersey: from its earliest settlement to the present time Volume 2.* New York: Kennard & Hay Stationery Printing Company, 1874.

# Acknowledgements

First and foremost, I would like to thank Dan McDonough, Historian, Town of Secaucus. I benefitted most from his sharing the wonderful photographs from his collection. During the years of working on the Snake Hill project, I have benefited from his help and suggestions. His knowledge and familiarity with "the Hill" proved insightful, and his patience and good humor have made him an invaluable friend.

I extend special thanks to Jay M. Arancio of Media Works. His valuable time and outstanding digital image dexterity during the scanning and presentation of the photographs proved invaluable.

Over the years Marcia A. Karrow, Executive Director of the New Jersey Meadowlands Commission, has been a good friend who encouraged my work and always offered suggestions that guided me to further information about Snake Hill.

Primary research in Hudson County was made possible by the help and cooperation of William LaRosa, Administrator of Hudson County Cultural and Heritage Affairs, and Paul Paradise, Hudson County Records Manager.

Thank you to Jon Crispin for allowing me to include two excellent photographs from his collection of Willard suitcases. Willard Psychiatric Center closed in 1995, and more than 400 suitcases were found in the hospital attic. With intense feeling and sensitivity, Jon was able to portray the personal belongings of those people entering the facility, never to return home.

I thank Andy Kazmierski, Photographer, and all who granted me the right to reproduce photographs from their collection.

A special thanks go to my cousin, Joni Aschoff Schumann for her valuable assistance throughout the primary research phase of the project.

I would like to thank my family, Scott, Evan and Cathy for their editing comments and technical contribution to this work.

Finally, my sincere appreciation is extended to Paul Rabinovitch, my Publisher, for his continued support and encouragement during the years of this project. His prompt response and assistance was always a constant source of strength for me, especially when it was most needed.

## About the Author

## Linda Aschoff Stampoulos, Ed.D.

Linda Aschoff Stampoulos grew up in the shadow of Snake Hill and as a child, played with her cousins in the salt marsh and on the banks of Penhorn Creek. She was born in Weehawken, New Jersey, a half mile from the entrance to the Lincoln Tunnel, and about five minutes from Snake Hill.

A child of immigrant ancestry, her maternal grandparents, Paul and Ella Frenzel, left Germany and arrived at Ellis Island in 1916. Having owned an embroidery business in Germany, they soon opened a shop in West New York, New Jersey.

Her paternal grandparents, Arthur and Amelia Aschoff were born in Hudson County where her grandfather earned his living as a house mover. He had seven sons, most lived in North Bergen. Grandfather Aschoff was well known in Hudson County, so much so, that the Township honored him by naming a street "Aschoff Place," where Dr. Stampoulos spent her childhood. After graduating from North Bergen High School (Class of 1964), she attended Montclair State College and majored in Education.

During her college years, she moved to Secaucus and worked in Eggers Delicatessen, a popular store in Secaucus. Upon graduation from Montclair State, she obtained a teaching position at Lincoln School on County Avenue in Secaucus directly across from Meadowview Psychiatric Hospital. Meadowview was built in 1929 and became the new residence of the patients from the Lunatic Asylum at Snake Hill.

She received her Masters of Arts Degree from Montclair State University which paved the way for her to teach both Research Methods and the History of Medicine in Montclair's Graduate Division.

After earning a Doctor of Education Degree from Teachers College, Columbia University, she spent the next 25 years with the Hunterdon County Department of Human Services. Dr. Stampoulos served as the Director of Alcoholism and Drug Abuse Services for the County. In the field of Substance Abuse Prevention and Education, she also served as the County Municipal Alliance Coordinator for fifteen years. For a number of years she was the County Mental Health Services Planner, and together with the Hunterdon County Mental Health Board and liaisons from Trenton Psychiatric Hospital, she prepared the County Mental Health Services Plan for five years.

Her publications range from the historical and sociological conditions among Native Americans to pictorial presentations of the Grand Canyon and the American Southwest.

Other publications are self-help books which tap into the visions of Black Elk and Joseph Campbell guided by Native American insight for recognizing the healing powers that surround us.

Currently she is retired and serves on the Board of Directors of Hunterdon Drug Awareness Program, a Substance Abuse Treatment and Prevention Education Agency in Flemington, New Jersey.

## The Author's Dedication of this Book

Hermann and Antonia Burgermeister were embroiders from Switzerland who arrived at Ellis Island in 1911. They had only one child, a daughter Ella whom they adored. As Ella grew, they realized she was feeble-minded (developmentally delayed) and would always remain a child. The Burgermeisters opened an embroidery shop in West New York and became close friends with the author's grandparents. In fact, they named their daughter, Ella after the author's grandmother. As the couple aged, they realized they could no longer care for Ella and having no alternative, they committed her to the insane hospital at Snake Hill. They went to live at the Fritz Reuter Altenheim retirement community in North Bergen. When she went to Snake Hill, Ella was only thirty years old and in good physical health. Although the author was only a child at the time, she remembers her grandmother being very upset at the news that Ella went to Snake Hill. When she asked why she felt this way, her grandmother replied, "Ella will never leave Snake Hill, and will probably die young." Her grandmother was correct. Ella died within two years of her commitment. The location of her grave remains a mystery. Yet Ella is not forgotten. And so it is with deep affection that this book is dedicated to Ella as a small token of love and remembrance.

www.ingramcontent.com/pod-product-compliance
Lightning Source LLC
Chambersburg PA
CBHW041702160426
43202CB00002B/10